I Approve of Me...

Sets Me Free

I let go of being addicted to my paycheck which allowed me to expand into my affinity for wisdom.

Robert Wilson

Editing by Amy Lignor

I Expand Through Life with a Forward-Looking Attitude

I am Robert A. Wilson with **Cowboy Wisdom Visionary Vitality**, and I am writing to introduce you to my "I Expand Through Life" seminars that are opening peoples' eyes to the innocence of life so they may discover their inner 'canonized' abilities with NLP and Hypnotherapy.

NLI means 'Neuro Linguistic Innovation,' and it's a new way of unlocking people's state-of-the-art insight so a person is FREE to engage and experience their dreams – turning those dreams into a reality, both in life and in business.

My "Expand Thru Life" Seminars have been truly well-received and avidly expand people's wisdom; sets free a visionary vocabulary that unlocks astute awareness by utilizing rhymes that authorize them to understand they can trust themselves to expand their wisdom, energize their 'wise' lying dormant inside of them, and unleash their entrepreneurial talent to experience life with galvanizing gusto.

With Unselfish Love in My Heart and a Sassy Smile in my Soul I Thank You.

Robert A. Wilson

Vision Statement

I now unleash people's heart supremacy to understand that it's the image of my dreams and my emotions which are the electricity powering my actions; they are the elevator to my pinnacle...

Wisdom is the key to be free innovation; it opens the door for me to soar and see my plush prosperity, viewing my oceans of opulence. I relish seeing me surfing on my seas of success, basking...

On my blissful beaches of unselfish love, and exuding my selfless admiration for life as I sit on my mountains of money...

Because I choose to embrace the images of my dreams with daring, self-starting self-esteem – now and forever!

Mission Statement

I now understand that the mission of **Cowboy Wisdom Visionary Vitality** is to open people's inner eyes with my words of wisdom; to unleash their trendsetting talent...

To engage in their innovative sage and expand their wisdom by unlatching the intra-enterprising wise; to set free their entrepreneurial endeavors forever...being free of the paycheck...

To realize life is living intrepidly – FREE everyday by playing in the fields of prosperity because people *choose* to allow **Cowboy Wisdom Visionary Vitality's** wisdom be their guide...

A guide into their promised land, as I now see the world spinning in wisdom, wealth, talent and magnificent money flow...

May_____

life flow in the lavish avalanche of copious copiousness, now to eternity, in the right way, in a loving way, under grace in a Divine blessed way, and in Divine order...**NOW!**

I APPROVE OF ME... SETS ME FREE
By Robert A. Wilson

For more books like this one, visit Robert A. Wilson's website at:
http://cowboy-wisdom.com/
2013 copyright by Freedom of Speech Publishing, Inc.

Printed in the United States of America
The publisher offers discounts on this book when ordered in bulk quantities. For more information, contact Sales Department, Phone 815-290-9605, Email:
sales@FreedomOfSpeechPublishing.com

Product and company names mentioned herein are the trademarks or registered trademarks of their respective owners.

Freedom of Speech Publishing, Leawood KS, 66224
www.FreedomOfSpeechPublishing.com
ISBN: 1938634098
ISBN-13: 978-1-938634-09-3

A SPECIAL THANK YOU TO YOU!

On behalf of everyone at Freedom Of Speech Publishing, thank you for choosing I Approve of Me... Sets me Free for your reading enjoyment.

As an added bonus and special thank you, for purchasing I Approve of Me... Sets me Free, you can enjoy discounts and special promotions on other Freedom of Speech Publishing products. Visit www.freedomeofspeech.com/vip to learn more.

We are committed to providing you with the highest level of customer satisfaction possible. If for any reason you have questions or comments, we are delighted to hear from you. Email us at cs@freedomofspeechpublishing.com or visit our website at:
http://freedomofspeechpublishing.com/contact-us-2/.

If you enjoyed I Approve of Me... Sets me Free, visit www.freedomofspeechpublishing.com for a list of similar books or upcoming books.

Again, thank you for your patronage. We look forward to providing you more entertainment in the future.

Acknowledgements

A heartfelt thanks to my Mom and Dad who
have passed for being my parents and the work
ethic and moral values they instilled in me. I
understand I wasn't always the easiest child…

I thank my family and extended family: Nieces,
Nephews, Aunts, Uncles, Cousins, Sisters and
Brothers for being a part of my life.

I thank every one of my friends for being a part
of my life.

I thank Amy Lignor
(www.thewritecompanion.com): published
author, editor, ghostwriter, reviewer, and a truly
dynamic writer.

I thank God, Mrs. Universe, the womb of
unconditional love and enterprising energies, all
people, spiritual ethers, metaphysical realms,
physical playgrounds, mystical magical heavens
of miracles, and all realized and unrealized

sources in the cosmos, for opening the way to authorize and allow me to experience my life, *my way.*

I thank all my listeners and guests on *Cowboy Wisdom NLI Radio* at: www.blogtalkradio.com/cwbywsdm.

I am thankful for Patrick Kungle and Girard Sagmiller with *Freedom of Speech Publishing* for all they do for me.

I thank everybody who buys and reads in order to expand their lives in a perfect way.

I am thankful for my life everyday and in every way, under grace in a perfect way.

I love life and life loves me!

Contents

Preface

This vision is written in first person, so when you read this read it as if you, yourself, wrote it.

To enhance my self-starting self-esteem, I expanded my vocabulary because I opened my prospering prowess to understand the words inner dialog; the words I verbalize are the life I live, revealing my prosperity consciousness.

Now, as people read this they will come across new words, never big words. Disallow getting caught up in whether I know the words or the words are new in order to allow the emotional energy of the words to engage my daily life with my sired desires. Because the words I feel will energize my dreams to be experienced in my daily life.

After I read this, I will pay attention to the words I was unfamiliar with; they will begin to show up in my daily life to expand my wisdom, energize my intra-wise to feel forthright and feisty in my life, allowing me to approve of me. This open allowance will set me free now and forever in a true titan way.

I write my visions in the first person allowing my subconscious mind to feel the energy to expand my life...

As I choose to read this, I understand the subliminal wisdom in this vision that will allow me to enhance my life – to flow in harmony with my sired desires.

Letting Go of Being Addicted to a Paycheck

I asked myself this question:

How will I feel when I realize vast wealth and infinite success is my new comfort zone?

As I now comprehend that colossal wealth and lavish success are my friends, I unburied this ardent admission and I confidently choose to cross my internal vast deserts of fear; letting go of my addiction to my paycheck and to swim my inner mosquito-infested swamps...

Of being scared to live without a paycheck – a fear that's buried in my body cell's DNA and society teachings; so, first off, I defined I am a defiant daredevil willing to ride hell bent...

For election across my vast desert of obtuse fears. To live without a paycheck is a scary abyss my fears tell me, but my steadfast capitalist brazenly tells me...

I am a visionary rebel riding at breakneck speed to expand out of want and need as my steadfast stalwart tells me I am living proof of being a 'goof-off,' as my brazen bullishness shows me...

I am being a lily-livered chicken-shit life, afraid to step up and out of the delirious doubt of having steady money...

From a paycheck that is unsteady because it is somebody else who has the control. As I look at the economic landscape today there is an unsavory atmosphere toward the workers...

In the world; this whirls a new admittance so I now choose to pay attention to *my* roads of riches. I see the insecurity of my paycheck now as I see my internal atmosphere is my sunrise wise...

Liberating my stalwart seer to ascend me into realizing I encompass the collaborating chutzpah, putting my saintly patience into my daily walkabout; to show me I have the calming clout...

To sovereignly untethers my sassy tenacity to swim the swamps with whomp-em stomp-em, kick the rotten crap out of my blundering listlessness that my paycheck addiction has wrought. Being too scared...

To confide in my facilitating fortes allowing my egotistical arrogance to play me like a fiddle just dilly-dallying around in the insane – feeling hokey singing karaoke, crooning...

The pains of poverty and never wondering how talented I am because I felt I had to have that paycheck; to live raised heck with my spirited entrepreneur for sure as I have awoken...

The sovereign conquistador, adoring my stroll in lavish never-ending luxury because I freed my heart hegemony to unlock my autonomous gutsiness...

To let fly my spry whetted wisdom, my unconquerable, intuitive, innovative wit; to lust in trust of my canonized abilities because I coldheartedly admitted a paycheck is...

A thief of my true trendsetting individuality, because I now appreciate my whetted warrior walking about the universe showcasing my cowboy clout, showing off my cowboy poise...

In my rancher facilities sanctions me; I relish the opulent outcome of my savvy safari as I devoutly declare "**I am a breed free of need**," so I am sitting down profoundly experiencing and tasting...

All my rich milk chocolate abundance, relishing eating at my copious utopian pudding, celebrating my lavish unselfish love Divine – grandeur divine – an inheritance of vast wealth and colossal success...

A bountiful buffet bar liberated from all sorrow that I borrowed from being addicted to my paycheck, then blaming bosses for my choices. This was my greenhorn silliness...

Now, as I ostentatiously open my internal discussion I can see a paycheck and job was ingrained into me from childhood to present day, leaving me over-thinking...

I must have job to live was a statement deeply rooted in my belief system, embedding all my faith in my paycheck for political correctness. It was to make me feel safe; to make sure my bills were paid...

As I was my employers 'puppet on a string,' with undertone worrying about everything. Joy – the essential we must all have to survive – was being put in somebody else's hands. It was security, yet it was also...

A discouraging worry, because my life was always in the hands of somebody who had the power of the 'pink slip,' I grasp now that one slip up from me and out came...

The 'pink slip' – whether it was a personality conflict, lack of work, or poor management decisions, the company fold all these mistrusts together and it played out in the back of my mind...

So now I understand a paycheck is really an unknown quality just as being an entrepreneur for sure, because everything is up to **me**. Every ounce of new acumen is a win for **me**...

To experience outright freedom being uncontrolled from the clasp of somebody else's hand; so I now understand what is, is not, and what…

Isn't is a paycheck that soothes the conscious mind, divulging my ingrained imprints of what I have been taught goes for naught in my real security to be FREE of being out…

From under the thumb of somebody else. But in the grand scheme of self-esteem my wealthy witem is the REAL security for me, so I laid out this new clout of undeniable reliability in noble abilities…

I realize whose security my paycheck really secures; it is the payer of the paycheck that every worker secures for sure. But the payer bears the brunt of everything, so let's be fair…

The paycheck causes a jealousy in the workers because they see all the payers' money coming without seeing the underlying costs that boosts for coveting feelings; so now I understand…

I am addicted to the ease of my paycheck because it's there every week, allowing me to do whatever I need to do is really the stew of 'Oh NO!" what I do with all my innovative witem…

Sitting on the bench causing stench in my enterprising corridors, impatiently waiting, baiting me with prospering premonitions that initiate an impatient capitalist cavalier; unleashing...

My entrepreneurial seer, endearing my heart to my hierophant supremacy. As I saw the people I worked around and hung around, the sight profoundly unlocked my state-of-the-art cockiness...

To step up and out onto the risk-taking dance floor, seeing my mistress of wealth and success across the way as I choose to sashay across to ask her to dance causing a riotous rapture...

In my internal debate of whether to go for it or just take the easy way, disliking my treks of wrecking my health with a FOR it realization, or do I admit...

With all the cutbacks, working three part-time jobs without making ends meet, which turns me into being coy; in dealing with the payer as I now realize the payer is the soothsayer player...

Of his/her dreams. The payer emits the blustery BS into the payees' dreams; I now coldheartedly admit the coldblooded truth that 'I am a paycheck puppet doing whatever the payer asks'...

But as I expanded to understand that I was addicted to my paycheck, I allowed me to say:

"The heck with that!" This was a revelation, and I walked out of the cave into Disneyland...

With all the rides being free, only because I decree that I am the man/woman to waltz in my dreamland extravaganza as I expand into showing me that I encompass the visionary valor...

To live my sired desires in a bold new way; in an unselfish, loving way; in a Divine blessed way; under grace in a picture perfect way, and in Divine order, NOW!

I Bared My Heart and Soul

Today I bare my heart and soul to unclasp my unassailable classiness to speak my unconquerable truth, to admit I did it and I am the **only** one who can do it. I humbly admit...

I am the only naysayer, dream-stealer, time-stealer, seer, wizard, noble, wealthy, successful, healthy cowboy/cowgirl experiencing my life in my inner corridors, because I am the one riding...

This spiritual horse across the plains of the mundane; to embellish this, I am the only listening and communicating student. I am THEE maestro magician of my Divine destiny, teaching...

My trailblazing boldness because I had the shameless brazenness to look at myself naked in the mirror; so now I enhance the world and all its inhabitants...

With award-winning wisdom, because I revealed my healthy heart and cooperating soul to the universe. This authorizes me to see everybody in the world as a teacher for me in their own way...

To expand my life, as I propel pioneer veracity in the world, to show all the people that it's

okay to encompass internal belief, but stop
fluffing the pillows to sleep in deeply embedded
dreams...

In the subliminal countryside to make it a soft
landing by telling the world what to do is the fly
in the omniscient ointment – adding the 'pooh'
in the stew lives...

In my innermost host/hostess that's authorized:
"I Am!" to open up to claim my fame today
because I ruthlessly admitted it was **me**
permitting the naysayers, dream-stealers and
time-stealers...

To get in the way; I let them cause me to wail in
fail; so today I held trial within me and
unemotionally come to grips with my wasting
time – the time I threw away listening to those
who have never done anything...

As I ripped out my dimwitted daunting despair,
I freed myself of doubt, sending it all into
burning flair. I watch the stack of ash go away –
now and forever – showing me and televising to
the world...

I encompass the canonized clout to be FREE of all crusty distrust.

So I was sitting and writing this morning when
my adversarial seer whacked me. It was a crack
like lightning...

The 'whip quip' Robert A. Wilson: I have been a rapping chicken crapper, flopping around like a fish out of water because I have been stuck in the muck of my mundane...

Because it was easy to stay alive in the insane of the same to my conscious mind, but my mundane way was a typhoon of turmoil....

To my subconscious mind; dreams sired desires, opulent outcomes, and my visionary voyage to expand the world by energizing peoples' innovative talents...

As I had to adamantly admit my egotistical brat, keeping flat on back, smacking me with my fears in my conscious and being scared in my body always looking for approval to move forward...

In life; locking my being safe in my subconscious mind stifled me. But now I am open to this brand new prowess that I was hiding in the comfort zone – going through the motions with all the wisdom and courage...

That is required to light the fire of desire in the world populace as Rob – you played in the fringe of success; however, Rob – I instantly admitted – this ruthless truth made me play like a phony pony...

I showed virtues on the outside and in the conscious, but underneath there was sneaky vileness lurking that would jerk my chain in vain; as I now realize virtue is my daring do...

Because I choose to see the world free of the rapping chicken crapper that used to hide from everything, going through the motions, telling the world everything I knew was me being daunt...

In discipline; this authorizes me now to be the daring disciple of discipline, to win – putting this straight into the public eye for people so they can choose to be FREE...

Because I have an honor – a code that I live by. I don't expect anybody to do anything I can't or won't do, so sending the heart-darting message to the world to watch people expand their sand...

To sail affluently, unlocking innovative love to flow from within them; this allows me to bald-faced concede that I allowed my arrogance to cover up my lack of wisdom for a time...

How have you/I used arrogance to cover up ineptness?

Every person on this earth has done this, but the ones that fly first class disclose the pitiless veracity to drink...

The smooth nirvana nectars of absolute love, copious copiousness, colossal success, and bountiful Divine bliss. Yes, I can write. Yes, I can do hypnotherapy, NLP, NLI – all of that and more. But to unleash…

My debonair flair, I must walk the trails of fail, because to wail in fail is me denying the wisdom of the world that flows to me from other people, causing…

My frothing at the mouth and the frightened clump of absolute fear to rise up in me, making me stop listening to those who make me uncomfortable in my inner empire; after I heard the things that zinged…

My ego I would say: "Let's go ___!" *(Your Name)* "Get the hell out of here!"

I have to stay in the same BS session with those who talked about what they were going to do with a snoot-full of beer, waking up…

The next morning searing with self-pity, admitting the ruthless truth which allowed me to say goodbye to my inner lies – the bratty fears of a scare-dee cat – do dat, do dis – whatever I could to waste time…

Telling people how busy I was caused a caustic crass blast in my wealth and success plan that was plain to see in my visionary veracity; so I say today in a new day with…

A new crack of the 'whip quip' that catapults me into assaulting my paltry contradicting habits, with forthright fortitude, with swiftness of a swarm of mad wasps; banishing...

All my unrealized despised vanities brought in front of my sired desired court; as my risk-taking valor is my judge, my empire-building boldness is my prosecutor, my gunfighter warriors were...

My jury saying goodbye to the lies my defense council told; saying goodbye to the dishonesty, to fly away as my court reporter is my temerity trust, in my gallant grit to address...

My internal landscape with hardnosed innocent fidelity; as I now understand the way to the Promised Land, I stop flip-flopping and procrastinating. I wrote a book of questions...

That self-assuredly caused me to look in the mirror with my heart and soul exposed to the world; as I now grasp to lead the world I choose to be:

FREE OF NEED, GREED, AND DERELICTIONS!

FREE of my outdated convictions, I unleash the sassy new decree that I am free to write, employ and embellish my rabble-rousing business plan; write to explode my marketing plan into...

The universal vista with the power of an atomic missile – sizzling with sassy, innovative, zillionaire zeal; this opens my eyes to realize I only failed because I allowed dream-stealers their time-stealing destiny; and unwilling...

To understand my dreams are my financial security. As the Union and electrical trade *(Your Business/Field)* was my own insecurity in the long run, but short term security...

Was my wisdom, will, and innovative talent; I expanded, and I now grip with intrepid trust; God, Mrs. Universe, the Infinite Spirit, mystical sources in the universe which all allow my miracles, and give to *all* people...

My innovative talent and my iron-willed titanium backbone – a brazen, baby boldness to see people succeed; this is the pristine scene in my inner sanctuary and it allows me to ubiquitously understand...

I was intentionally put in places to move me forward – to say goodbye to the dream-stealers with a heartfelt 'thank you'...

And say 'hello' to expanding the world and opening peoples' eyes to their innovative ingenuity – to my $30,000 per month cash flow...

As my cash flow coming from all seminars, hypnotherapy clients, speaking engagements –

they all say: "Welcome, Robert A. Wilson.
Come right in, sit right down and let's have
some tea to celebrate your newfound freedom.
Rob, you shall enjoy life now. Let us deploy our
lust for life, allowing people to feel a lust to
trust in their audacious abilities, by authorizing
them to employ *Robert A. Wilson's Cowboy
Wisdom* that was earned by being willing to
fail."

It was earned by having the guts to say 'I failed'
because I disavowed everything. I now open...

My whimsical wise to realize there is two guiles
in the Universe: One; I dial the guile denial
which is a delusional pollutant caused by my
unwillingness...

To admit the ruthless truth..."I don't know."
This opened the way for trade winds of wisdom
to blow bold, lively, omnific wisdom into my
state-of-the-art landscape; to cognize...

I knew a lot about everything but lacked the
intricacies of the business world; outright I am
bright in everything now. I am allowing me to
rainbow bright...

In the intricacies to unlock blocks of love,
wealth, success, perfect health and Divine
inheritance, dance in the Universe of other
people's wisdom, to waltz internally...

Seeing daily omnific magic instantly appear in my scamper, un-hampering, expanding people's lives and appreciating the instant revealing of my $30,000 per month cash flow...

Because I am willing to admit my ruthless truth about every microcosm in existence in my inner scenery, opens my physical phenomenons to mirror my glowing inner scene...

As I feel, smell, taste, hear, see and touch, the keen serenity of lavish luxury, I sense the salt air freedom that blows through my inner seas of ecstasy...

In every phase of my life; in a bold new way; in an unselfish, loving way; in a Divine blessed way; under grace in a picture perfect way, and in Divine order, NOW!

Dreams are My Mistress

I now grasp the concept that my dreams are my
mistress in the night opening keen insight into
my phenomenal psyche; unclasping the
connection to my physical world opens my
clairvoyant clearness...

Brashly blasts my fearless rocketeer seer into a
stratosphere of première prowess; to adhere to
my fortune-teller foresight ignites a frontier
scout with clout that unravels all doubt...

So I instantly let go of my fright to take flight in
feisty whimsical wit; invigorating, gutsy, hell-
raising, thunderous omnipotence captures the
rapture...

Of my revered reveries, as my way of life
allows my vivacious visions to telecast my
'Broadway Show of Fantasy Feats'; this has
unleashed my lust for my luxurious utopia that
sent me twirling...

Into my core inquiry; to look in the eyes of my
dreamy mistress unsheathed my majestic
inquisitiveness, seeking and uncovering the
intra-trendsetting, rabble rousing...

Effrontery savant savvy that opened my
explorer eyes to see the world as my stupendous
stage of sagacious sapience of life; because my

dreams are my imagination, sensations are brought forth enticing...

My lust for life and lighting up sassy tenacity in my soul's desire; lighting the fire in my heart's hegemony opens my eyes to see...

My dreams are a mistress in the night; she entices me to rise and shine as I open my emotional eyes to see dreams are **me** daring **me** to be FREE in my daily life; this undoes a newborn buzz...

Lusting internally yet flying externally, letting go of the internal and freeing external encumbrances, I gallantly grasp that I encompass the grit and get to energize my knight-errant adventurer...

To romance my mysterious mistress in the night realizing my daring dreams make me let go of being scared; this expands me out of my fears and expands me into Xanadu-woo, grasping....

Dreams are forever expands fissures; my affixations change. I leave the mundane that is society's insane way of controlling my dreams; this is gone, like today's dawn opens my eyes...

To see life is a mistress: Beautiful, bold, unique – she's always in motion and mirrors my imagination. As I unlock the blocks of fear, the mistress of my dreams becomes real in my mind's eye...

Because I am spiritually spry, flying into my dreamland and understanding that a mistress is inner enlightenment, fanning my flame to fantastically animate mystical epiphanies...

To see me sitting on the beach communicating with my mistress of the night in a white Divine light, beaming so bright that it emblazons my amazing, magnificent innocence; naturalizing...

Galvanizing, gallivanting rants of revolutionary autonomy, niyama, temerity, spectacular as I dance with my mistress of success and expand me from playing in the world of worker-bee fears...

Opens my eyes to liberate myself – for I was working really hard to stay where I was, but now it is time for me to instantly scat like a cat – be FREE of any society scarcity tracks; this authorized me to crack...

The poverty conscious code and leave my footprints of canonized wisdom in stones on the Earth for people to read; a creed of confidence to leave the mundane, mildewed, unharnessing my fun...

In the sun parvenu doo, letting a cowboy yell to pell-mell give it hell – the debonair flair that allows my words to flow and cut through the mumble jumble of anxiety, speaking to my mistress of the night...

In cool, classy, caballero clarification; exposing
my hometown hero I poise...FREE of know it
all noise as I speak lionized libretto, showing
my mistress of night...

That I am the knight in shining armor. You can
hear the 'whoosh' as I swept her off her feet,
showing her the world in a flashy dash, beaming
urbane fame...

Because I unmasked the crass in my innermost
landscape promptly showed me my jovial
jubilee in every facet of my fantastic daily life...

Because I unlocked the lock, setting free my
cowboy 'get up and go' to show the world I
whirl in opulence; I stroll in rebellious
liveliness; this is a visual decree that I am
dancing with mistress of night in daylight...

Of my success, showing me I am 'walking my
talk' with assiduous action, because my mistress
recognized my gallant chivalry to stir my clear
emotional elixir, invigorating a fire in her
heart...

To dart vibes of the visionary intuitive,
energizing my emotional hero because I
embraced my inner mistress with a heart full of
untutored love and a soul full of the
unconditional...

Because I let out venomous energy; I let go of
vindictive expressions, expanding into untaught

love, opening vibrant expressions of luminary omnificence virtuously...

Electrifying luxurious opulence – vivaciously enjoying my ballet with the mistress of magnificence all because I opened my eyes...

To realize the mistress was within me; she authorizes me to see when I open my soul, eyes, heart, or ears to dance with my cyclone of courage unhindered...

My intra-prizing wise unleashed my inferno of entrepreneurial spirit; now I swing with my mistress to open my eyes – stop ambling in ambiguity and engage in my gamble to have a ball waltzing...

With my dreams; romancing my mistress is the key to my kingdom; I am my own paramour of mysteries; I am at the top of my mountain of money, showing...

The mistress of my desires my name set in the marquee that lights the universal sky, beaming a bright knighted sword of sapience that cuts through the lies of life...

As I now comprehend, I encompass the guts, gall and give all mettle to feel the financial love from the Universe beaming back at me; I feel my heart glow, my soul beam...

My savant ego strut, showcasing a stouthearted
stallion as I show me the way to wealth that lay
in my beaches of bountiful bliss...

In a bold new way; in an unselfish, loving way;
in a Divine blessed way; under grace in a
picture perfect way, and in Divine order, NOW!

Embossing Emperor

I now understand fear let my Embossing
Emperor admit I was scared of life and unlocked
my revered resolve to relish everyday
simplicity; this opens my luminary bravery,
engaging....

My innermost savvy and strengthening my
intra-evolving, visionary, omnific legacy
invigorating my natural sincere intuition to flow
from my subliminal shrewdness, authorizing...

My knighted sassiness to grab my trampy
dispiritedness by the seat of the pants and the
nap of the neck – tossing the crappy character
into the compost pile, turning...

The paralyzing pig-headedness into scampering
sapience; so, in this instant, I expand out of
being scared; this stoutheartedly sanctioned me
to dare **me** to be FREE in every way...

 As I choose to dare my heart hegemony to jump
right up and throw my silly, scared deadbeat out
the door into the fires of freedom to never ever
be seen again...

As I begin the brand new adventurous
extravaganza, I take a stand of who I am – I am
grand in my one man band that's accompanied

by everybody in the whole wide world, twirls
this pearl pureness...

Un-harnessing my typhoon of triumph because I
encompassed the guts to ask this quantum
question:

How am I scared to experience life?

This unlocked my robust boldness...

Setting me FREE to see I was a scare-de-cat
brat looking everywhere, unaware that I should
be looking in a mirror to see my heart
hallowedness; to write my native name...

In the marquee lights of the Universe, showing
people it was alright to be scared as I proved to
all the people, and me, it was in my highest
grandeur to admit I was secretively terrified...

To exuberantly experience my dreams was me
impaling my intuitive innovativeness without
realizing my disdainful disgrace was laced in
my deepest inner fabric...

As I instantly understood that fear circles the
surface of my conscious mind; as I now come to
terms with this admittance, I was secretively
petrified in the subconscious mind...

Stopped myself from experiencing my affluent
aspirations; because I now grasp I was in misery
by repeating my history, this unsealed

everything and I let go of my internal his-tory. I admitted...

I was scared. This purified my rare, revolutionizing, audacious revelations, expanding my daily excursions through life because realizing I was scared pleased my uninhibited me...

As I unlashed my dashing, esteemed picture of my lively leadership to the world, I forthrightly admitted to being nervous and freed my idolized audacity to see the situation with the eyes of an excited sage...

Sagacity, as I win, in my honed heart hegemony authorized my warrior wit to be victorious in communication. I am THEE Pulitzer Prize Winner in listening. This realization broadened...

My majestic maturity and amplified my pathfinder Diviner, showcased my titanium backbone within me and broadcasted my shrewd self-assurance to the world, highlighting my heartfelt confidence...

To walk into the Universe exposing my chutzpah; because I now comprehend, I am a rare breed, boldly revving up emotional enterprising decrees to grasp...to ask the question:

How am I scared of money?

Stopping my internal apparatus when I first asked that question shut down all internal quackery.

I was driving back from South Dakota when I got internally blasted with a sharp premonition; my speaking, writing and *Cowboy Wisdom NLI* was about leaving a legacy for my nieces, nephews, great nieces and nephews, and so on...

So they can choose the life they desire. This lit a fire in my belly to blatantly love living. Yes, I am a living legacy, displaying my gunfighter will to step into the streets of trust showing...

The world my lust for life after watching the youthful exuberance of the youngsters turn my head to run straight ahead; to where I am choosing to win to leave my family with lavish financial love...

Leave the Universe streaming with my wisdom, sagacity, and moral nobility; to show the world that when I was scared I turned red in face – I turned tail and ran back to my comfort zone...

Like a bonehead, dreading everything about the choice as I felt safe in my scared haughtiness; to feel safe was easy – all that was required was to live life by the definition of insanity...

To do what I have always done, expecting different results which insulted my entrepreneurial spirit; it kept me hiding, wishing for more as I snored away in the same mundane place doing...

The same thing, making **me** *disappointed* in **me**; so I hid inside my melancholy follies by golly; I obstinately stayed in my humdrum world, the same in my conscious mind, just staying...

The same and sabotaging my pioneering spirit along the route; allowing my subconscious mind to sleep; latching me in attachment to my cantankerous calamities of knowing everything about everything...

Left me behind, singing in the inane pain of pity that I loathed, deteriorating my self-esteem and condemning my will to win so that I became insanely impatient with **me**, so I unsheathed my kapish...

By choosing to jump off the couch, grab a fighting bull by the horns and set him on his rear end, ascending me into audacious, amazing brazenness to finally understand the bull was scared; it was me...

So when I jumped up grabbing the bull by the horns, I flipped him over; I am now sitting on the bull as he looks up bewildered, mirroring my always wanting to run back...

To safety whip up pure burping fear, being
scared in all phases of my life as I choose to go
crazy in my mind, blowing wizardry instead of
laziness; so I showed me that I was radically
bold...

Unleashing laudable leadership and sending all
the BS of the world into a giant compost pile,
converting negative BS into a powerhouse of
electricity, lighting the world up...

With visionary vitality in a robust reality,
because I choose to employ my unalloyed
loyalty to myself to show the world a way to
live unscarred, with a suave aptitude to open my
life...

To see the world in unselfish ubiquity; to be
alright living in the bright lights while moving
around the Universe with an open ear to hear
and pure eyes of clear confidence, to be in the
moment, seeing...

The energies of the world as I expand through
life, exuding emotional electricity from my
heart powerhouse, as I energize the Universe,
the Universe diversifies my wise to realize
people...

With different points of view I un-skew new
portraits of prosperity in my immaculate
images; steamy romance prances and allows my
kingly energy across the Universe, setting
free...

My queenly serenity to quietly unlock my
feminine divinity within me, as I see my paths
are clear – my life is pure spiritual omnipotence,
as I now understand my virtues are vital...

To experience my tidal waves of wealth and
success in my inner sanctuary; this liberates my
glorious nucleus of pious integrity and allows...

My moral magnificence to shine as I relax in
never-ending lavish luxury in a bold new way;
in an unselfish, loving way; in a Divine blessed
way; under grace in a picture perfect way, and
in Divine order, NOW!

I Expanded Out of My Self-Taught Fallacies About Money

I asked myself this question:

Does money give moneyed-up people an arrogant attitude, or does my perception of how moneyed-up people act grant them their arrogant persona?

I now fathom the distinct disconnect people encompass when it comes to money. Because people associate arrogance, control and corruption with money, culturally embedded myths and self-taught fallacies...

Undo the buzz. I stopped thinking about what I would do with all the money in the world, ruthlessly admitting I would lose it and be unhappy, simply because I lacked the astute wherewithal...

To handle that much money; so now, as I coldheartedly admit I lack money cleverness, this opens my optimistic oracle to valiantly broaden my shrewdness about gigantic sums of money...

This illuminates my sunlit wit to understand money opens my heart hierophant to listen to people validate my wisdom about money; to escalate my innate prowess to cognize money is a potion...

That puts my 'Life of Riley' in motion; as I now relish my life with free flowing wisdom, galvanizes my intrepid innovation, my stat- of-the-art talent soars, engages my visionary valor...

Electrifying my shark attack action and empowering my lavish, endless, cascading cash flow; I now understand, as I undid this ultramodern realization about money, I can have fun and I am having fun...

Because I focus on what makes the money; therefore, more money is forever flowing to me in order to enjoy my 'fun in the sun' bliss that money brings to me, because money is an innocent lotion...

That soothes my ride through life now and forever; understanding with ascending astuteness, intuitive woo and canonized abilities, I know there always will be – in all ways – more money...

Then I require; this thought streams into my life experiences, unlatching this brash modernization to recognize that cash has been the way, and still is the way, people put the rich on a pedestal then get mad at them...

When they do what is right for them, with
people out of the loop thinking wealthy people
do underhanded things to get ahead; but in all
realness, wealthy people make choices...

For the highest outcomes, then when well-
heeled people are in the news and across the
media spectrum doing underhanded things...

Wannabe rich people choose to be in cahoots;
ordinary people forget their morals, doing
disgusting things to their fellow countrymen to
gain status and be seen by rich people...

This causes havoc for all involved – mania
which never gets solved because the emotional
outrage rages on and on; because forever in a
day people make choices – money first is the
worst case scenario...

A scenario unimpeded by morals as people try
for the money; their emotional landscape is
scared to death, bringing up all their horrifying
dreads from previous experiences; then money
is blamed and shame spreads...

Through their inner landscape like a prairie fire
irking the ire, as raw hard feelings are exposed
forever. Money is innocent, yet taking the brunt
from people's...

Egotistical rampages – people unwilling to
admit "I don't know." As I now unashamedly
admit in my emotional energy these words, I am

expanding into understanding mammoth sums of **fun** money now...

As the higher social order of the world always has flashed their arrogance, flaunting and embellished by the media to make sure that everybody knows who the wealthy are...

The wealthy people make sure the rest know; "I have money. Thus, I am better than you paltry people." Peevish writings and events of history speak about money...

In truth, people who have gained their beliefs and faith in money from books and ingrained vanities pertaining to money are living in the same old paradoxes of poverty consciousness...

People of the world, and I, have been taught about these values, leaving us all fuming, stewing and distressing inside because faith and beliefs aggravate these already ingrained disdained imprints deeply...

Entrenched in people's inner scenery, spinning the same money game, keeping the scarcity story going around in all levels of people's minds. For me, this ends right now! I end it! I...

Expand out of that crock of crap to amplify my new avenue of animated affluence; unlocking the locks to the fact that money is innocent frees a new money spree to understand money is grand...

As I choose to expand my acumen about money
I free me from bullying bosses who cynically
say 'I will fire you or do something unsavory' to
the employee, as well as the acquaintance on the
street...

To make people feel diminished under their
snobbish stare causes people to squirm, and
makes the immature wealthy person look
weasel-lee-wormy...

To karmic cosmos, people, and me, as they
chuck their myopic smugness around in front of
us, throwing their weight around and imprinting
a false impression that it was the money that did
it...

But in reality it is immaturity by an immoral
baby with money that lacks people skills that
does the bad, so they end up silently shutting
down their money flow because by the time...

An arrogant person understands the money flow
has stopped, it's too late; they have a date with a
'going broke' destiny. Then they get the thrill of
going down and asking the people...

They terrorized for a hand out, looking at their
once victims with pitiful begging eyes; they
have to grovel in heated humility and eat that
humble pie that tastes just like crap, which
unravels the gallant insight...

Every enterprising business owner should remember...people energize their wealth, prosperity, and cash flow; the people always have this insight embedded in the subliminal movie in their mind that people can take...

My money flow away instantly. A word of advice? Stay humble with employees and patrons so the money flows in – a glowing, lively, omniscient windfall – today and every day in a bold rushing way...

To disgrace people with wretched arrogance backfires; people with mature money abilities never flaunt their cash, only raucous rookies taunt people with their power. Money itself is...

A bountiful blessing of energy, but money in the hands of a narcissistic tycoon is simply a buffoon heading for a rude awakening; the acute acumen is...never associate money to immature tyrants...

People see that money buys justice without realizing that it's weak morals and ethics that allow money to run lives, so people encompass embedded dread towards money...

Because of the asinine arrogance and powers to be put forth, then speaking down to the people who actually make the country run unlocks the common sense that working people are...

The everyday locomotives energizing the bottom line of the economy, authorizing the money to flow from bottom to top. Money is just like building a skyscraper...

Have you ever seen a skyscraper started at the top and built down?

This opens another question: In building a money making enterprise, what is the foundation of the money flow?

This unfurls the heralded conclusion that wisdom begins the innovation empire; building talent invigorates the enterprising endeavors...

Wisdom brings in the money to run the economy which starts with production – placed into the workers' hands; the economy relies on the bottom line of a corporation; today the powers...

To be are so concerned about corporate profits they forget people elected them – not a corporation. That is yet another nugget of common sense. This world has become...

As I now understand ideologies, a way to paralyze the economy; It is just the source of exchange for wisdom, innovative, substance and talent that's needed to achieve success, so stop blaming money and look...

At the actions of the people with money; it's always people with conceited cockiness who flaunt their way of life and money so selfishly in front of the people to energize their cash flow...

To all the people who encompass large amounts of money, the people you look down upon are the ones that keep your cash flow going; when people think more about money...

Than they do people, what happens within society is the top ends up at the bottom; I open this prosperity prowess as I expand into new paradigms; the shining diamond for me is...

To realize I encompass the wisdom to expand people, realizing everybody in the world understands one thing I am unfamiliar with and they can do something...

I am unable to do; at this time a rhyme chimes in my sublime mind that everybody in the world is divine to trine all of our wisdom, innovation and talent to ballet the world...

Into nirvana newness, opening peoples' minds to it because people with money act so arrogant and think people who work for a living are below them, leaving people with subconscious hate....

For money, because people tie money to people rather than have the fortitude to understand the fact that money is never responsible for someone's actions. It is fun to watch people...

Who have money, or get a promotion, then see their egotistical arrogance shot up like a rocket being launched, this allows me to realize the real rich people look at the world...

With a philanthropist eye – as wannabe rich who itch their arrogance and chirp about themselves as a real rich person, talking to people about their life as a wannabe rich person talks bad about...

The people who work for them, blaming them for everything that goes awry in their business, spewing disingenuous words...

To cut the workers morale to ribbons; then the workers start talking amongst themselves to paralyze the work for that one day. I have witnessed this...when people allow money...

To be the gage of their success; they live in an arrogant cage of rage that is their real enemy – people I now realize money comes from expanding my wisdom, energizing my inventive innovation and trusting...

My titan talent to idolize my abilities. This allows money to be the elixir I stir in the pot of what I got – what I asked for because of my forthright foresight to enliven the lotion to put in motion...

That money streams **in** from people who trusted the enterprising entrepreneur for sure; as I now grasp this I stop paying attention to moneyed-up people, seeing them as nothing more than awesome-gurus...

To teach me the ways of money...showing me ways money can be fun; to travel the world expanding people's lives as I stop to realize that wealth is the energy of wisdom, innovation, talent...

With stouthearted stubbornness that gleams from the heartfelt supremacy living in all people. So stop bitching about money. Stop complaining about rich people. Unleash my dashing craziness...

To pay attention to my state-of-the-art intentions – to sashay down my own paths of prosperity and pay attention to everything that expands me as I walk my roads of riches paved in shiny gold bars...

As I now sit on my pedestal of copious cornucopia in a bold, new way; in an unselfish, loving way; in a Divine blessed way; under grace in a picture perfect way, and in Divine order, NOW!

High Winds of Wisdom

Good day!

A good today and everyday in every way –
forever, there are revolutionary high winds of
wisdom blowing brilliantly across the earth –
swimming in the atmosphere – dapperly
divining...

The trine of spirit-body-mind and awakening
my snoring, strong-willed sapience within; it
begins today, and forever there will be a never-
ending mystical omniscient resolve evolving
from....

My core décor, freeing the world of despair as
my debonair flair caresses the negativity of the
world into auguring energy, generating astute,
tantalizing, innovative visions every day...

To play like a baby in the universal vista,
vigorously initiating playful persistence,
aggrandizing my intra-prizing wise and ripping
the mask off all negativity with sunrise
perkiness that unfurls...

A savvy utopia – a revolutionizing prowess
inspiring spectacular, enthralling acumen for
people to latch their dreams to; energizing their
'get up and go' to glow in the flow...

Of financial love; optimizing willing wittedness
to expand into their preferred conduits of
collaboration as I grasp the fact that

I Won!

I won with whooshing, omnipotent, nu-clear,
peerless proficiencies ...

Because I now fathom everything in life is a
guide to ride the tides of prosperity to my
beaches of bountiful abundance, introducing
blazing and amazing hierophant intrepidness;
galvanizing...

Hell-raising revelations; invigorating nirvana; a
daringness that is embedded with optimistic
feisty willingness that ignites steadfast
declarations of oracle magic to stream serenely
– quietly revealing...

My breezes of easiness that enter my internal
landscape, open my trendsetting scenery to
realize life is about expanding out of the gloom
of antiquity into miraculous magnanimity...

This features my spiritual ingenuity, realizing
my daily meanderings enhance my yearning to
'YES!' everyday alchemy, revving up natural,
incredible galas...

Personifying the gleam of my self-starting self-
esteem electrifies my 'full steam ahead' vow;
embeds a 'get it done with fun' attitude and a

fantastically unified newborn stateliness that
sees every sunrise...

As a new surprise of superstar, ubiquitous,
rabble-rousing parades; realizing my innate
splendor enamors my blazing, amazing gusts of
robust trust to bust through my inferior barriers,
heralding...

My brand new acuity as I now look to canny
cleverness to energize my innovation, to
showcase my talent, to relish and experience my
lavish, never ending, surging currency
currents...

To embellish my unrestrained superfluity
because I now realize that when I do things for
money it turns into a financial fiasco; I realize
disingenuous...

Stuff happens when I allow money to be my
master; it turns into a moral, ethical and
financial disaster, because I let money be in
charge of me rather than my moral heart and
ethical soul...

To be brazenly rebellious I take the sagacious
trails allowing my cagey wagon master to take
me over the mountain passes, liberating my rich
prospering percipience because I now realize...

Moral intelligence wins in the end, because
farsighted insight energized the whole kinetic

caboodle of free-flowing rivers of copious riches; when I do it to expand...

The world's wealth, wisdom brings success – an unselfishness money acumen that finds me because my contributions liberated my distributions, magnetizing my utopia upshots...

To set me FREE authorizing me to uncover and discover mother lodes of wisdom that broaden the worldly vista, allowing me to take siesta's on my seas of ease, surfing...

My oceans of pristine serenity as I enjoy the view from my magnificent mountains of money that I now reside on; viewing my voyage I choose to undertake, I realize I started this with money...

Which was my focus at first – then my savings was whisked away because I was paying attention to the money, thinking I could do it all myself because I had my big-O-ego...

In high gear without realizing I was smearing my fearing – scared to expand my wisdom – scared to death to admit what I didn't know transformed me into a gerbil...

On the spinning wheel inside a cage; I was going as fast as I could, mirroring a cow chewing on cud, everything in motion without any emotional input or output from me...I was just flat out; the lights were out...kaput...

Like soap on a rope, just hanging around being washed away to my dismay; so now I energized my chutzpah, catapulting exulting exuberance to dance my...

Hallowed, untraditional, trendsetting zeal – pulsating astounding hegemony into the universe's vast craftiness; to unlocking empire building desire to fire on all cylinders of spiritual horsepower...

Showering the world with illuminated innocence, allowing people to open the eyes of their soul to see their newfound freedom within their innovative skin, sanctifying kevalin inspiring nativity...

To arise from their terra incognita reservoirs-hors-concours; to apprehend the awesomeness of their lives – FREE of competition in the physical; to allow their heart's supremacy to reign...

Ornate optimism through every phase of the amazing adventures; endearing others to their life escapades allows me to rest on my beaches of quietude with a dynamic attitude, showcasing...

My astounding accomplishments achieved **only** by strolling through life as a whetted warrior – a savvy student – a Toltec Teacher maestro that gets on the horse to ride hell-bent into the lands of wisdom...

To win within my skin, seeing **me** as the self-starting savant – FREE of wants and needs – to engage my emotional sage betrothed my heart and soul to walk down the aisle...

Of moneyed-up matrimony, showing the world the collaborating ceremony of my wisdom by marrying my breezes of boldness to fly around the world in a Lear Jet, relishing...

All the pristine paradises in a rich regal way; in a bold new way; in an unselfish, loving way; in a Divine blessed way; under grace in a picture perfect way, and in Divine order, NOW!

Avant-Garde Witem

I am setting FREE my avant-garde witem,
showing the world my wisdom, innovation, and
talent that energizes my mammoth money flow
to fill my prosperity accounts, now and forever
in an overflowing way...

As I beam my visionary luminosity, buzzing my
courageous curiosity that honed my heart's
heroism, I instantly send massaging messages,
paint pictures...

Of my magnificent, electric maharishi that
showcases my statesmanship in the skies; that
portrays my awakened soul's smile and
ascending my chivalrous chi expresses...

My silver-tongued veracity, cutting the ties to
violent communication which un-tethers my
sovereign seer from my fear – introducing the
world to a non-violent communicator;
synergizing my soul's serene, linguistic walk...

Intuitively modernizes my daily extravaganza
bonanza delighting my inborn savvy; sworn to
calm communication I unleash my awesome
awe, televising my audacious wisdom and
energizing...

My rivers of resolve, igniting my keen-witted wizardry unsheathes my kevalin kapish to realize success stems from unstaining my stained thoughts ingrained from childhood tutelage...

That when things go awry, it was because I did something which was the dimming thought processes learned; I turned...I learned to approach my life situations with those inbred dreads that people...

As I now grasp things, I realize I once approached my daily life with a stifling assumption that I **had** to do it the way everybody else did to avoid being in the line of rigorous ridicule, slowly pilfering...

My requests to embellish my life of lavish abundance, making me feel lesser in blessing by darkening my dreams with extreme mockery from society's hypocrisy, my courage to admit...

My ruthless truth that, when I get mad, angry, or frustrated, those feelings tell me I am insecure in my abilities to communicate new – in the moment – because I just expanded universes...

I now understand change; I heal, create, and understand transformation; I have expectations to comprehend using these words once kept in a closed box – paradoxes that keep people thinking small, living small, following...

What somebody else wrote in a book, hooking
people in the mundane rearranging of furniture
in their minds – thinking they are going
somewhere. In coldblooded truth I admitted...

I was basically in the same place from 1998 to
2009, until I began speaking, visualizing and
grasping to expand, that is limitless – I am
limitless in my innovative energies,
triumphantly turning on...

My emotional powerhouse; enterprising my
intra-innovation moves into the movie of my
mind's eye as my valor galvanizes utopian
tenacity and cultivates everyday new astuteness,
culminating...

Intuitive temerity 'Yes'-ing my yearning to
discern dapper, inborn sassiness, catapulting
everyday realness, naturalizing my lordly lore –
for sure, I endear me to my vanguard path...

As I ride through my universe's diverse
landscape, understanding life is an experience of
events, inventing new ways to broaden my
rainbow essence by painting my colorful
charisma...

On all the horizons all over the world; to
'whoosh' soothing lotions of love and optimism,
my trendsetting intrepidness opens new
sensations of fascination to flow through my
veins of fame, fostering...

Amazing magnificence and exuding fluid lucidity that lubricates the earth's ethers with an attitude of quietude that excites my plainspoken confidence, cutting the intense density of chilling darkness...

That lurks in the corners of **me** – the darkness I tried to hide and cover up so nobody would ever see the real me; but I just came to a coldhearted realization whenever I tried to hide something...

My moral and ethical subconscious mind knew it, so it blew the whistle on me as I thought I walked away FREE and clear. Because I chose to look around, I never saw anybody...

So as I was in a scurrying hurry, I unlatched this premise which sanctions my sanctified grandeur to stand right up to grasp – with unselfish steeliness – **I** encompass pure cleverness to comprehend....

The magical eyes of God are always upon me, as the soothsayer ears of Mrs. Universe hears me all the time; so now I grasp the mystical airwaves that carry my unique vibrations that embrace...

My personified harmonics; so God, Mrs. Universe, the Law of Abundance, the Infinite Spirit, and all the Mystical Sources in the universe and cosmos, people now see...

What I do, and my sublime morals and ethics
are with me 24/7, summoning everything I
require to keep my squeaky clean spirit clear in
my inner hallowed honour...

Candid understanding is what I now grasp; I
always dance like nobody is watching, but
always act like everybody is, authorizing my
moral nobility, embellishing...

My valorous ethics to prance my enhanced,
emancipated, niyama, hallowing, amazing
nibbana celebrations – inflaming sumptuous
splendor opens my front door and comes right...

In, sits right down, as we talk about the luscious
luxury life allowing me to swing in my
esteemed paradise, rousing my regal essence to
realize NOW is MY time to live in my Promised
Land...

Sauntering in my colorful charisma, canonizing
my billionaire bounty, televising my
humbleness to nestle in my posh villa,
appreciating me for my candid willingness...

To understand wisdom, innovation and my
talents; this allows me to sleep in lavish luxury
every night – to play in my pastures of profuse
profusion...

In a bold new way; in an unselfish, loving way;
in a Divine blessed way; under grace in a
picture perfect way, and in Divine order, NOW!

Enterprising Entrepreneur For Sure

I asked this question:

How free do I feel when I let go of being a businesswoman/businessman?

I see I am an enterprising entrepreneur for sure all the time...

Energizing my intra-wise, feeling forthright feistiness, unleashing my pert pioneering essence to showcase my innate potentate power to the world; to excellently exposing...

I am an enterprising entrepreneur for sure, I will endure my trials of turmoil and relish in my trail of triumph. By unlocking this new premise I now understand businesses go under...

When they plunder around looking at the bottom line they panic about money; this opens my effrontery eyes to recognize that businesses go under by pandering to their biggest clients...

While skimping to their newest clients without cognizing that every client is equal; as business keeps its eye focused on the bottom line, they latch on to the bigger clients...

While they may slight their smaller clients – as
that client grows they start throwing their
business at the competition, because the
business forgot to be an enterprising
entrepreneur...

Instead, they remained status-quo, being
screwed-blued-and tattooed, then thrown out the
door; the money flow slowed because the eyes
were on the old...

Instead of resting half on the old and half on the
new, so the wise tale of fail is to keep the eyes
on the new, caring for the old as hearken heart
hears all, sees all, and keeps harmony...

In the flow of the glow rather than opening up
the innovative intuition to expand their state-of-
the-art business tango; as a society we have to
be taught to shrink...

In times of challenge and to be lavish in the
good times, as I now realize as soon as a
business becomes financially challenged they
turn to cutting prices – nixing their financial
frequency in the world...

As I now grasp, finances are a fickle trickery in
the subconscious mind because the whole world
has been taught to cover up and close down
when finances become tight. Yes, slow down...

The spending but open the visionary valor to
unleash a rabble-rousing resolve to evolve into

an enterprising visionary, optimizing luminary vitality and energizing...

An internal inferno of innovative ingenuity; because I now see this from my experiences – the more I focused on money the less money wanted to play in my life...

Because I finally expanded into understanding as I cut prices, my wealthy wisdom winces as the Universe in convinced that I lacked the sassy audacity to win my game of life...

Because of God, Mrs. Universe, all the mystical magical sources in the cosmos – my magnificent miracles to all the people in the world were not seen by my unconscious; the genius grasp that...

When things go awry, they must, to awaken a savvy spryness within people. It is easy to fold and go home, which I have done because I was scared to go in any farther, I darted the real...

My life held fear that never went away until today, because I now understand the fastest way to being on the losing end is give into everything I have been taught, everything...

I know because that is where the world is today – dismayed with k-no-w way to go; as I now realize, I fell into this deviltry because that is what I was taught that brought me all the trouble...

As I now realize, when in trouble I must double-down on my profound facilities that will give my silly wanting imp an instant dose of silence, allowing newness to saunter from...

My dauntless daredevil, giving me a quick whack of wisdom, a swift kick of gutsiness; as I now realize, every time I failed I gave in; when the first eccentric challenge showed up...

To dupe me in reality, it was me, unwilling to listen, expand, or energize the gallivanting genius within because I absolutely had to know before I could go forward – this way of thinking thwarted all opportunities...

To win because my egotistical arrogance upset me so badly I was glad to get away – head back to being a paycheck puppet; as I now comprehend, when a challenge ballets...

Into my life it authorizes my divine diviner to attend the ballet – to blatantly ask in a lively loving way for the challenge; to express new tantalizing cleverness...

To allow me to uncover and discover the new, astute, potentate prowess being explained to me in a colorful canonization of my sovereign savvy, because I now am open...

To realizing money has never ever broken a business or a person; it was disconnect in the person because they focused on the money, rather than the real deal which is...

The lack of wisdom, innovation and talent to expand into new money; as I now ask how do enterprising entrepreneurs try to hold on to all its customers now, rather than stop and go out...

To get new customers to open new cash flow, allows me to ask how is my largest customer also my biggest liability? How is my smallest customer my new biggest customer?

Holding on is a bond, but how is holding on the biggest downfall of every company? As I open my eyes to realize holding on cuts down new profits, a business cliental mirrors...

A merry-go-round, because to be successful a business has to be detached from the client, allowing old to leave in order for the new to enter – realizing the smallest client has room to expand...

And the largest client may be as large as it will ever get. So now let's untangle a dancing dare to grasp the fact that most companies going under pull this blunder; they get complacent...

In the enterprising expansion, and when they realize it is too late, they have been bitten by the 'bah-humbug' bug; they were asleep at the wheel, forgetting the wheeling and dealing...

Instead they took a nap, allowing somebody
who was awake at the wheel and had the
hutzpah to deal them out of the poker game of
life now and forever, got rich…

All entrepreneurs have this bug; money is first,
second and foremost, which makes an
entrepreneur toast – and die – instantly; so now
I unleash my avant-garde witem, electrifying…

My wisdom, innovation, and talent; they merge
to create my never-ending, mammoth money
flow that allows me to glow, filling my
prosperity accounts now as I walk my tropical
spectaculars relishing…

My oceans of opulence as I sit so comfortably,
watching my waves of peace and prosperity in a
bright right way; in a bold new way; in an
unselfish, loving way; in a Divine blessed way;
under grace in a picture perfect way, and in
Divine order, NOW!

Pleasing Everybody is Selfishness

I now have expanded into asking myself these questions:

How is trying to please everybody selfishness?

How is shamelessly receiving appreciation and acceptance unselfishness?

Now, ultimately, "I just deserve..." "I am just worthy of..." These unmask my heart's temerity...

To the coldhearted truth that I tried to please everybody and then said, "No, thank you," as friendships suddenly tanked, cutting us off from each other...

As they said, "If you don't do this our friendship is over," I went into a panic for a nano-second, before saying, "goodbye" to my phony friends – which authorized me to admit this coldblooded veracity...

A **true** friend **never** says anything like that; only lonely, superficial friends say those words, so let the phony friends come and go. After all, the quicker they leave and go on their way is better for me...

As I never allow them to play in my life again;
so when people have to have somebody do
something for them, it is really their immature
peevish image of themselves...

In their subconscious mind of money and wealth
that's saying that, because I see it in the world
with the images of war torn countries – they
have a subplot of wealth. As I now expanded
into this, the images...

I see of money and wealth taught to me over
time were disparaging, making me scared of
money, wealth, and success, because even the
wealthy have an image of going back...

To the beginning that causes them to hold on
even more tightly; those who give back stay on
top, and those who put a stranglehold on life fall
back to the bottom. Money has been taught in a
negative manner...

To keep people in fear, through images and
scissor-bill media, the outside look proves how
well a person is doing. There are other
sides...look what this person is doing...

Look at the lottery winners and how they
suffered because of the money instead of saying
they didn't understand money. They went
through an unwinnable challenge because
money entered...

Into their lives, but people forget to enter into the energy of money which is a double-edged sword; one swipe of the razor sharp blade and I cut away the poverty in my life. The sharp blade cuts...

Into my morality because I become arrogant and stuck up, cutting away my friends and family, or I give too much money which allows me to now understand that anything that goes awry...

In my life is because of me – my unwillingness to expand into the wisdom and energize my emotional fortitude to put the image of whatever my emotional spunk and guts say into action. I comprise the wise...

I realize I broaden my inner landscape to feel I belong in the wealth countryside because wealth is for everybody; it is the inbred image, the innermost intelligence, heart, energy, soul...

Sapience – all that I have to expand into the millennium of money which unlocks this primetime paradigm that money has been the same since the beginning of time. So is the way people view money...

However, money stays the same as people's interactions with money become nothing more than the way money plays in their life. Opening the soul to see the outlandish utopia ahead, love flows to me...

Because I now totally grasp the fact that lavish amounts of money wait for me to broaden my brilliance; to radiate the innate vibration that makes money feel right with me...

I now understand, Robert Allen Wilson, *(Your Name)* can stop chasing money; I have the guts to expand the inner landscape and unleash my heart synergy, unsheathe my soul's tenacity...

To magnetize the earth's ethers with a classy persona – so classy and awakened that money rushes to fill my bank account now that I have stopped chasing money; I have stopped eavesdropping on the world's snazzy shrewdness to feel...

The cosmos is nine months pregnant; with all the wealth and success I desire, it lights a fire in my mature maharishi to realize wealth and success are grand, but the real grandeur is, in fact, sharing...

With the perfect mate; this knowledge authorizes me to date my love, enter into my Shangri-La holding all of my desires; because I now start all my intentions in the heart, engaging my soul, energizing my gut that struts...

Awakening my listening lionhearted warrior and brining him into my daily life to hear the sagacious seers speak to me, as I now agree it is by listening with my heart – with sired desires fired-up...

That my majestic mesmerism tantalizes all my divine grandeur to come a running at breakneck speed, because I now realize selfishness is about serving others and leaving...

Myself out, crying doubt, saying; "Look at what I do for them and they do nothing for me!" That has happened to me. Then they think my life is their life, embedded with stumbling strife...

In my dreams – oh, yeah they would pet my ego and pat me on the back as I went splat right in front of them – trying to make them happy. THAT is my definition of selfishness now...

I tell the reader...Doing for others by sacrificing my own dreams and allowing them to control me is my definition of selfishness...

Un-scared, my daring revolutionary effrontery produces my magical understanding of unselfishness – it is to embark on my heart's extravaganza, being the leader of my band...

Of rainbow revelations, to understand that money, wealth, success, love, grandeur and divine inheritance awaits me in Terra Incognita Paradise as I choose to no longer fear my sagacious titan...

To saunter into realizing that living my
preferred paths of prudence was never ever
selfish, because I now realize the 'ISH' of my
life opened my striving soul to see it is my
Divine right to be a knight...

In shining armor, riding into lavish luxury,
because to expand the world I realize I come
first and foremost; thus, I encompass the wealth,
health and wisdom to send forth shameless...

Sapience with conduits of – "I can do it!" I
allow people to see what I was yesterday; it is
like viewing the Industrial Age, and allows all
the people of the world to engage...

My sword carrying sage to cut lies – to fly –
facilitating luminary Yahweh by saying 'YES!'
– by applauding hallowed wisdom and
electrifying heart thaumaturgy; illuminated and
in charge...

Of my intra state-of-the-art escapades that pull
the Ace of 'I AM' in the rich palace of my life
because I choose to understand the way to make
money. I choose!

In a galvanized gala, I love outright, blessing
every day with my rays of robust awesomeness.
I am spry and alive – living my plush prosperity
in the right way; in a bold new way; in an
unselfish, loving way; in a Divine blessed way;
under grace in a picture perfect way, and in
Divine order, NOW!

I Approve of Me

I now relish the disapproval from those who have never done anything – thinking they know everything – embellishes my kevalin approval of me that sets me free with my eyes open...

As wide as the universe, energized my polished pluck because now I understand disapproval from nincompoop naysayers employs my sumptuous success to beam straight to me instantly...

As I no longer restrain my fame and fortune hunter to saunter into the happy hunting grounds of enterprising endeavors, I unclasped my classy cleverness to declare that:

I am the winner of my game!

A game of innovative playfulness because the more those two-faced disgracers disapprove of capitalistic collaboration, the more my endless esteemed flow of bounteous abundance appears from...

All sources in the cosmos, unsheathing this snazzy new premise; I now look at disapproval from worrywarts as approval that I am expanding my canonized confidence, energizing...

My intra-state of the arts – a Promise Land
Dexterity – because I stopped lusting in needy,
sleazy greediness and stopped subliminally
blaming money and all my life events for
everything...

I turned to lusting in the titanium trust of my
awesome abilities to say there is a God; look all
those sheep that disapprove of my way of life;
however, God says: "Way to go!"...

To abound in profoundness, my mind now
understands that I am fueled by the thrills of my
warrior shrewdness – the gifts I unleashed when
I chose to quit looking for approval from the
scissor-bills ones...

They talked about everything they were going to
do while crapping their pants in scared-dee-cat
fright; out one side of their mouths comes
blame, hefting the blame on everybody for their
life situation, playing...

The victim out the other side of their mouth; this
process allowed me to realize I looked for
approval from couch potatoes and I unlocked
this block to understand sibling rivalries were
stored away sneakily...

Standing in the way, because as a child I was
seeking approval from others; then, when the
approval came in the form of a comparison or
criticism...

I promptly went silent – I walked away dismayed; however, to show I was a tough hombre I kept my chin up, while inside I was harassed by my pride because I really wanted approval…

That ingrained enigma that always kept me wondering why things were happening to me – why I was seeking approval from outside sources; as I torched my internal apparatus…

With a fussing mustiness, I now realize the way I got my way was by playing victim, looking for sympathy and living apathetically until the instant I opened my omnipotent heart, releasing a darting…

Daring revelation through my inner landscape that told me to stop coddling my dope on a rope Snidely Whiplash crass, which caused me to caustically crazy in laziness. The more…

I understand the sibling, the stuff unlatches the ruthless truth within me, setting me free from existing in a childish sheepishness to allow me now to understand all that happened to me. I realize the ingrained disdain…

Dissidence, but really it is me buying into being a victim of the circumstance that prances down the aisles of ill-dilly dallying despair; as I implanted these messages…

As real truths, because my family members said it was so, I caused a mosey-doo merry-go-round of drama in my subconscious mind; because I now understand things my conscious mind blows off...

My subconscious mind grabs hold of an imprint I chose to live by in my daily life, so these embedded dreads from my childhood grasping on were family members doing and taking things...

Calling me names, sending disrespectful verbiage and actions my way as my family, friends, or just chance encounters said and did things they thought were funny, actually...

Implanting needy-weed seeds to grow later in my life; because I now encounter the same situation than that situation I thought was nothing, ends up sabotaging me from walking into...

My Taj Mahal; instead, I crawled into my bed of dread pulling the covers over my head to never be seen again. This is where I began again until I my thrills to waltz into my Taj Mahal were unveiled...

I now encompass all spiritual savvy, physical prosperity, unconditional love with a significant other that is mystically magical – my world is pristinely phenomenal...

To walk while understanding that I am the effrontery expander of Xanadu in the hearts of people, opening the world to understand peace is the kapish of lavish avalanches...

Of affluent abundances; I allow people to embrace their childhood with Robin Hood chutzpah; by untangling the wreath of wrong I felt internally and ruthlessly, I realized I bought that into the world in the first place. I was taught...

By life to be a victim, so I dislodged myself and found a nirvana where I will be the Robin Hood within my skin; I take my kevalin knife and cut the ties to the lies of my childhood, unraveling...

My traveling, trendsetting temerity to recognize I am the clever prodigy that has the hegemony hutzpah to harmonize my childhood with my dashing dreams today...

To reside in my land of milk and honey; as I see me basking in the sun of multiplying money in a rich robust way, I choose to be okay with the disapproval of many who were afraid and tried...

To rain on my parade with a crass charade, like they cared about me, which was a lie; so I show them – I paraded my wisdom, innovation and dreams right through...

The front doors of the nagging naysayers and
went to the backdoor, made a u-turn to walk
right back out the front as they swore at me,
telecasting their soured doubt...

So I now reside inside my willingness to look at
disapproval as approval, with a keen ear to those
who have walked where I choose to be a
peerless ear to my internal seers...

This sets me free to dance in my 'Broadway
Show,' glowing in my gigantic, luscious,
omnipotent wealth – now to eternity – as I thank
Mom, Dad, siblings, my internal seers, my
super-conscious...

Soothsayer's supra-luminal luminary's friends –
all the people in the world – as well as God,
Mrs. Universe, the womb of the Divine Order,
the Infinite Spirit...

Mystical sources and my magical miracles, for
playing in my continuous NOW – in a wild
wonderful way; in a bold new way; in an
unselfish, loving way; in a Divine blessed way;
under grace in a picture perfect way, and in
Divine order, NOW!

Self-Indulgent Habits are Poisoning My Life

From now to eternity I realize my own self-indulgent habits are poisoning my life; they were stealing my dreams and annihilating my self-esteem; because I feel positive in my conscious mind...

The unforeseen happens, setting off my secretive corruption, cracking my selfish haughtiness wide open in my subconscious landscape to now totally understand the haunts...

That did have viral emotion – an affliction within me, causing a caustic reaction inside me saying: "Shame on me!" for invoking self-inflicted cruelty before drifting into shift, jamming...

The shams of blaming somebody else for my life's circumstances right up my nose, as I instantly sensed the quick banishment of my dreams that were exiting my interior scenery...

At a high rate of speed; because I invoked the poke of self-serving selfishness, embedding the dread of want, need and greed, I felt my kidneys fill my bladder; the overflow allowed me...

To pee out my scared skepticism to bodacious-
lee speak this new creed:

I Am THEE disciple of discipline

Winning my self-esteem Kentucky Derby,
embellishing...

My Temerity Triple Crown Winner veracity; so
I opened my prizewinning-wise to recognize I
was justifying the lies of my self-pitying,
mindless saboteur that banished me from
living...

In my land of lavish luxury because I still justify
the lies of yesterday, comparing me to other's
way of life, always having me speak silly,
shameful nonsense like: How come other people
are so lucky?

My incredible integrity very blatantly told me
that my attitude sucked; being ruthlessly honest
with myself allowed me to understand the
poison that chides my revered reveries and
hides...

In my subliminal mind; so when I get all revved
up to take over the world feeling bold, brilliant
and enterprisingly vibrant – to outspokenly strut
my intra-prizing stuff, feeling...

Trendsetting tuff...until I came across my first
stimulating snafu that was to unlatch a snazzy

new acumen, opening my entrepreneurial acuity to see the open road of opulence ahead, but...

Instead the situation pried open my daunted doubter and activated my hidden rancor from a previous episode; I consciously thought I was rough-n-tuff and full of the right stuff...

In a previous situation that ended up having me quit my twittering, my nit-witted silliness to the world is against me, venom that shattered my self-esteem. Then I tainted my learning lesson...

With an exterior coat of 'I am smarter than everybody' – leaving egotistical toughness that internally scared me to death. So, now, whenever I feel I am better than somebody who is my tyrant, toxic and poking me...

In the butt, I play the King/Queen Butthead of my life and wallow in my conceited condensation that condemns my dreams; because I now understand...

The first thought and the last thought that flows through my internal landscape have lingering effects on the outcome, everything else is now like the Rose Bowl Parade – all looks good...

To the world; the winner of my inner Rose Bowl, shows me I am the poised player in my life as I open my heart stalwartness to admit I am the one poisoning my dreams...

With ingrained comparison I immediately look
at other people's lives, justifying my place in
my current life opens my eyes to understand I
am intoxicated with my upbringing even
though...

I thought I had all my negative occurrences in
hand in my core corridors, it was a bogus whoa
– I was telling myself this, but buried deep in
my core torso was the programming from my
childhood...

As I was taught, I thought my belief system had
to hold on to my dread, or feel they were
betraying my indoctrinated way of life; but I
now grasp everything – I require to live...

Today and expand my wisdom; I am now
sharing my brilliant ideas, televising the fact
that I understand my self-repressing habits and
self-deprecating beliefs, the selfish control...

Self-seeking expectations that I had, deliberately
expecting everybody to do everything my way
assuming things will go my way all the time and
believing...

It's my way or the highway, is poison to my
freewheeling wisdom in dealing with life's true
adventures because that old thief – Mr.
Expectation – raises its boneheaded
bogusness...

Stopping me from investigating my internal Wall Street; to invest in my dauntless dreams, unleashing my daredevil entrepreneur to realize...

All the wisdom I require is sitting in my subliminal sapience; it is hiding behind the blindness of my egotistical arrogance just waiting to be energized...

By me through eavesdropping on mystical sources, listening in my daily voyage to all I encounter, paying attention to the visual messages and hearing my sagacious sage authorizes...

My awesome audacity to ask myself this question: How do I allow family, friends, society, and outside sources create my personality?

Sanctions me to ask myself: How have I poisoned my life striving so hard to look good in other people's eyes?

How have I avoided looking in the mirror to see that I AM the Queen/King of my kingdom?

As I comprehend that I allowed the toxic symbolism of the secret societal order to dictate my way of life...

To cause me strife in every phase of my life because the first thought in my mind was what

other people would think of my idea; then, the
last thought, was what if I failed – tells me
today...

That when life-expanding quizzical questions
enter my innovative landscape, I must stop and
query the fury of these questions, because until
they are expanded out of bare heart my daunting
doubts will cloud...

My mind very loud, admonishing my abilities
and linger – festering up like an abscessed tooth;
I must unblock this until the infected tooth is
pulled; if not, the pain will continue to exist,
subsidizing the toxic quitter...

Within me because it's easier to quit; this
realization opens my eyes to grasp quitters
through fits, trying to get people to feel sorry for
them as winners smile, unleashing a gallant
guile...

To dial daring, intuitive sassiness – loving the
energized journey through every situation –
because winners stoutheartedly sanction life to
be an infatuation of sensualizing omnific
wisdom...

To recognize that life will wheel and deal every
day, expanding episodes – this knowledge and
plan to cease and desist from is required to light
the fire of desire, authorizing me to live inside
my esteemed dream stateliness, showing...

The world that as long as I address the internal poison, I let go of being thrown into the melting pot of bucket calf society, expanding out, not being hooked and booked in being...

A paycheck puppet, but expanding into being that effrontery entrepreneur for sure and energizing my enterprising endeavors to experience life with galvanizing gusto – keeping my prosperity eyes...

On the prize without giving a hoot about what's going on in my 'today;' because today is always a day of electrifying my savvy sagacity, being okay with my surroundings...

Because I now understand that, like an impacted tooth, everything is one step at a time; embellishing the well of who I am and slamming the door on the poison in the physical world; allowing...

The poison within my skin to slither out the door authorizes me to soar, singing my song I magically market my wares to people all over the world, watching them let go...

Of their own internal poison and expand out of their physical toxicity into their sired desires, energizing their cascading cash flow because I glow of genuine, lively, optimistic wizardry...

Because I now grasp that I encompass the guts to admit I had poison in my system and toxic moronic arrogance in my life, I go through the intra-evolving resolve to unshackle...

My canonized cockiness; to understand the poisons in my system I begin with food I eat, the books I read, what I write, and people I surround myself with who are visionary savants to sense the intensity...

Sensational sagacity enthralling my spiritual vitality, enriching peerless clearness to see my life flow in opulent opulence to beam a bright bold ray, reveling...

In utopia, relishing my flow of financial love in never-ending lavish avalanches of affluent abundances in a bold new way; in an unselfish, loving way; in a Divine blessed way; under grace in a picture perfect way, and in Divine order, NOW!

'Poor Me' Itches My Bitchiness

I now grasp the concept that my 'poor me' itches my bitchiness, just as my 'rich me' says: "Just shut up cowboy and get it done!"

I now realize leadership begins with astute listening everyday to discern everybody's real sapience, harmonizing individual prowess to learn every day, augmenting determination and allowing real savvy to emerge, innately galvanizing...

All my facilitating foresight into every situation; taking my 'know it all' blather out of the situation and allowing the wisdom from all to invigorate a mastermind ball, enthralling my rollicking...

Bullishness to admit to get it – that I fit in my emotional oceans of omnipotent opulence – to prance in zealous valor through my smiling soul, appreciating that I encompass the 'I have it all' gall to...

Effrontery, expand through life extravaganza by superbly striving in awesome liveliness to understand the situation as the 'poor me' wants to itch and bitch, stitching me into a paralyzing paradox...

Of 'pity me' poverty; as I now realize that 'poor me' sucks, keeping in the crux of paycheck correctness, sucks me into feeling sorry for myself – pilfering dimwittedness is dismissed from...

All phases of my conscious levels and sends this new way of living into my prosperity wizardry as my 'rich me' says the mantra of shut up buckaroo and get it done now; as I display...

Me, I expand through life with a forward-looking attitude to fly first class, lassoing Yahweh 'YES'-es in my heart of light brightness; to understand to live my Divine right, I dare...

My divine diviner to entertain my fame and fortune hunter, to look into the eyes of upbringing and see everything I thought was absolute as my entitlement dementia that allowed me...

To mention my intentions are the outcomes I facilitate; so when I look for entitlements the 'poor me' accepts what somebody will give me is simply my life causing strife...

As rifle-demeaning slurs are sent at those who set intentions then stop looking to somebody, unblemished by dementia; polishing their prosperity prowess to shine...

In divine daringness authorized me to see my 'rich me' pointing the sumptuous thermosphere and know it was a limitation because that's known to man, so my 'rich me' says there is more beyond there...

So now I boldly go over there where my dreams are waiting for me – to be there in a debonair flair to unleash my gallivanting genius, un-shrouds...

My crowded thoughts, the clouds allowing me to ride the cumulus clouds and bask in the sun's rays, for raving waves of wit, wisdom, innovation, talent, animated visionary éclat's...

Into the universal airwaves, astronomically inciting rich windfalls of affluence, vibrating effrontery sassiness that unlocks Mother Earth's awesome surplus to revolutionize opulent newness...

Opening majestic innovation, catapulting laudable lively yearnings in the enterprising ethers, allowing people to feel the nomadic nirvana enter their subconscious landscape to feel...

The peace of prolific everyday ardor; canonizing entrusting ambiances of accomplishment unblock my treasure chest of investing in me to be FREE, realizing I feel...

The sensations of success internally idolizing
my waltzing wisdom, the wisdom that flows
through my veins of ordained omnificence,
understanding life is a journey of living in the
vibrant frequencies...

Of **me**, emceeing decrees copious copiousness,
expanding me into my incredible intentions with
a simple 'goodbye' to the 'poor me' in a loving
way as I holler 'hello' to the 'rich me'...

In my breezes of boldness as my 'Rich I Am'
says: "Come in. Sit right down and let's drink
some tea because we are FREE to roam the
world"...

We are FREE to speak our epiphanies, gallantly
grabbing people's affluent attention with our
wonderful world of winning witem; this means
wit, innovation and talent, equals money,
because I shake, rattle and roll...

With my daily events, preventing people from
doing anything to me because I now grasp my
challenges and the fact that they are my
comrades; harmonizing amazing, lavish luxury
every day naturally...

Generates elaborate enthusiasm in my soul to
see outright utopian love, which lubricates
omniscient vitality, envisaging the
sagaciousness of the universe, entering my
lusting landscape to feel life...

As my mistress, magnetizing intrepid trendsetting realness every day by synchronizing sprees of sovereign prowess and enlivening my escalating energized savvy...

Culminating astonishing luminary accolades, tantalizing intuitive nibbana by gyrating my raving craving to see people expand their entrepreneurial frontiers...

Unleashing their wizard-seer to unthinkingly foresee my trails, hailing my heart-ascending intuition by listening intently, nurturing genteel zeal appeal...

To stream from my esteemed soul – doling out defiant optimism lucidly, lore fore-sure, igniting naked gallantry to see me walk unarmored into my daily life with boundaries confidently down...

Televising my unconquerable spirit, invincible iron will and my vulnerable verve, because I realize boundaries are fears and scared to embrace the 'something' I don't know; relishing...

This coldblooded veracity; they are telling me 'new' wisdom – how to achieve my cornucopia utopia – and I pamper myself with the 'plush' to feel the amorous ardor...

Of the universe melt my cells into heavenly peace, as I now reside in posh paradise. Geewiz...I now understand that I am the RICH: I am MY Rich I Am, says shah-zam man...

Let's go over there and lie in my hammock to view the mountain magnificence, as well as the pristine valley of peerless paradise – all this because I rolled the dice on my risk-taking friskiness that allows me...

To surf my seas of serenity in the right way; in a loving way; in an unselfish way; in a Divine blessed way; under grace, in a picture perfect way, and in Divine order, NOW!

I Admire My Spunk

I admire my spunk – to admit I have 'gunk' authorizes me to unstrap my crap to rap; to admit, I get it to invigorate sassy tenacity to tell the world to follow me – I will show you to the top of mountain...

To glow like the North Star on a clear night as I instantly take flight in my Divine light, gliding through the universe with my listening lithe to realize I am the man/woman with the grit-n-get...

To admit life loves me because it throws challenges in my way, to open my potentate prowess to 'WOW' me; to authorize my emotional wise to be the guide galvanizes...

My utopian innovation that enflames my effrontery explorer, to dare me every day to expand my sand to see many novel vanguard declarations flow from my internal inferno of entrepreneurial vigor...

Electrifying my defiant savvy to surge with emblazoned courage, to rise above the vain of the mundane and to realize instantly I un-spunk my 'gunk' which spins me right out of my funk...

To unlock my blocks of cocky cleverness, to
silently expand my omnific omniscience to see
the world turns in opulent opportunities – tuning
my emotional harp to play…

I unstrap the crap to rap as I comprehend my
real astute percipience, steaming from my
esteemed pioneering landscape that boldly
speaks unique acuity that wakes my sapient
soul…

To dole out dauntless, omnipotent, luminary
enlightenment by unsheathing my spirited glow
to blow winds of wise, intuitive nirvana;
discerning simple ways to robustly rouse...

Folks with carousing confidence; give them the
ability to walk into their daily escapades and to
stop playing charades in their internal scenery;
to unravel their parading prowess to 'WOW'
themselves…

When they look into the mirror and see their
liveliness gleam rainbow sassiness, it authorizes
me to realize that the more omnific and
enlightened I am, the more I am allowed to
unhook my ass-of-mine arrogance…

As I sprayed WD 40 on my egotistical rustiness,
I unbridled my stouthearted shrewdness within
me to realize that my stuck-up silliness was me
derailing dreams…

As I now appreciate my ego-busting conquest, I became arrogant thinking that telling the world its problems made me a transformational healer; I comprehend that I was squealing about...

My internal limitations; so now, as I open my energizing-wise eyes, I see I was really embellishing my challenges and nothing else, so now I show people their adventurous spark...

To hark their canonized journey, to live their dreams, because when I first began my spiritual conquest I thought – "Look at me! I am a life coach! I know everything." These thoughts sanctioned me...

To shut down my intra-prizing, expanding, emotional apparatus – exposing my winning wit while in reality I was as bright as a burnt-out light bulb by thinking...

I was going to tell the world how to live; I was left stinking in my thinking, finking on my inner acumen. Now that has passed like bad gas as I Omni-Potently open my heart smarts...

To grasp that I brazenly unleash my rhyming resolve to understand that NOW is the time I say 'goodbye' to thinking I am special, expanding into realizing...

I am unorthodoxly unique, encompassing luminary life with expanding insight to walk in public, recognizing all people as my equal,

energizing my common sense bravado to
intentionally...

Speak exceptionally optimistic words,
embellishing my sanguine emotional feelings
about everything and everybody because I
choose to electrify the world with sagacious
sagacity...

Rather than defy by trying, saying, and thinking
unsavory words or opinions that clogged my
inner landscape – now I have unclogged these
pigheaded bogus bog holes within my skin...

Cleaned out my whining, trying, crying in my
beer BS; because I realized today I was only
trying to go where I desired, I unleashed this
wham-bam-thank-you-ma'am moment in my
inner wizardry...

As I said to 'thank you' to Mrs. Universe, I said
'goodbye' to my trying ego; as my ego cried my
heart sang with visionary valor and, cheered, my
feisty philosopher said:

What the hell took so long?!

So I book the look of success and took the path
of triumph, unleashing my unconquerable
vulnerable 'oomph' as I have been showed the
way to play...

In my endless lavish fields of financial love,
unsealed my spirited savant promptly cognizes

my entrepreneurial eyes and they have opened
my heart's supremacy; I have engaged my state-
of-the-art audacity...

Now energized, my trailblazing entrepreneur is
standing tall; I allow my free-flowing financial
love to enter my life...

As I strive to be the savvy student; to hear the
world speak to me and listen to my inner, awe-
inspiring augur that expresses thaumaturgic
ingenuity...

To see the fact that life is a miracle – I am a
miracle magician within my skin, as I am THEE
mesmerizing maestro of my destiny; with a
triumphant smile I teach the world my rhyming
realness to allow...

All the people to feel their forthright fortitude
beam from within their skin, as people of the
world and I realize it's the right time for the
populace to be the prosperity leaders...

Of the world – to show the powers-that-be how
the cow eats the cabbage – sending their goofy
garbage down the sewer drains as all the people
and I unleash empire-building desire, lighting
the fire...

To free individual avant-garde enterprising
innovations, escalating the world into a
whirlybird of gigantic wealth unfetters the
stranglehold of the moldy old secretive few...

Allows the people of the world to expand their
epitomizing élans into omnipotent peace and
prolific prosperity through listening and
communicating ideas to be people who play
wise every day...

All over the world, sending the war pillaging
and plundering into pulverized compost to never
ever awaken again so all the people of the world
and I can begin with a new understanding...

We all win our game of life because we choose
to communicate innate innovations now to
eternity, as I feel my rivers of lavish luxury feed
my oceans of utopia I kiss every day with
kevalin purity...

I am relishing my ride through life. With a smile
of bountiful bliss I say, "Thank you God, Mrs.
Universe, all the people and my core décor of
luminary lore for all facets of my life."

In the right way in a loving way in a marvelous
blessed way under grace in a regal rapturous
way In a bold new way; in an unselfish, loving
way; in a Divine blessed way; under grace in a
picture perfect way, and in Divine order, NOW!

Omnific Talent

The coldhearted truth is I am unsatisfied in my heart supremacy. With the realization that I encompass the omnific talent to dance in the world with my wisdom, comes admitting to myself that I can get it now...

I have discovered my niche in speaking; I tell people they encompass the talent when they choose to expand out of being addicted to a paycheck, saying heck with my daily routine...

So my intuitive woo chimes a rhyme in my subliminal mind that now is the time to shine, divining my prime time wise to step up and begin to win by expanding wisdom and innovation now...

Flat out admitting: "I Don't Know Which Way to Go;" so now I look to the Universe for the teachers to un-preach the teachings of society and to preach the teaching of entrepreneurial realness...

Because the guru-truth is waiting for me unscarred, my heart does not fear my soul to ask the Universe to bring forward teachers that allow me to sing my songs of success; to waltz in wealth...

To bask in riches; to say "It's okay, Robert Allen Wilson *(Your Name)*" to dance in the world of wisdom, wealth, success, unselfish love, Divine grandeur and lavish, Divine inheritance...

FREE of being attached to a paycheck – to be coldblooded honorable with Robert Allen Wilson *(Your Name)* paychecks get my dreams in check NOW; what the heck? Let's spin the world like...

A top, unleashing my enterprising wise to lavishly lust in titan trust of my abilities to sit through the tuff times and to relish the Divine time in all facets of my life now – as I strive to teach people...

To see how their paycheck is holding them back, because I now realize a paycheck is easy in the egotistical mind but a torture to a spiritual dreamer...

Because everybody encompasses dreams but allow the extremes of the day to steal their dreams, because people put money first instead of expanding into the wisdom...

Then invigorating the oceans of innovation within them, energizing the enterprising gutsiness and then doing what it takes to win as I now realize this was my biggest downfall causing me...

To crawl...I was afraid to ask for outside wisdom to waltz in, setting declarations of modernized inventiveness, being finessed from the core collaborator and stepping on my 'get it done' accelerator...

I am now awake. I was addicted to my paycheck because every time I stepped out on my own I soon ran back to my mundane comfort zone; as I now understand there are many excuses I use...

Defusing my willingness to step up, rather I stepped back, slacking off and pissing me off as I backed away from the challenges instead of smacking the challenge into a grand slam home run and running...

The bases – receiving bountiful affluence and sumptuous effulgence as I see life is fun again; as I now realize I permitted my egotistical arrogance to run my life causing me strife in every level...

As I now grasp arrogance is being afraid to listen, unable to be taught anything new, and forces you to keep your head down. When I talk to it now, I say that I already know whatever is said...

Of my life because I forgot to allow my spirit, heart and gut to be the players with my mind sitting bench getting slivers because they are

unable to deliver the hits to get it; this
unleashes...

My dashing brashness to show the world this
time that my spirit, heart and gut are the players
in my game of letting go – of being a paycheck
puppet – expanding out of...

My current situation and occupation with
exaltation of my grit 'get up and go'; throwing
my prosperity party and energizing my
illuminated witem to get-em; to relish my
winning...

My freedom from my current situation with
galvanizing gusto; I never sat down and wrote
out everything I was going to go through
because I bought into the concept of 'ask and it
is given' as if it was true...

On some things and untrue on others, such as
understanding wealth, money, success, wisdom
and innovation are my quantum entities I
required to succeed in my affluent adventure...

As I now realize I lacked the understanding of
these vitalizing vivacities of these internal
entities because the enemies of these winning
traits were within me...

As well as electrifying my trendsetting traits to
experience my sired desires full array of sun
rays allows me today to grasp before beginning;

I choose to sit down and express my gallant valor...

Of my visionary vitality with newborn get-em witem, allowing people to use this insight and outside sources are the light of wisdom I required to light the fire of feisty inquisitive...

Resolve, evolving enterprising veracity by optimizing laudable vitality and instigating my heart stalwart to step forth onto my roads of riches that I now realize are mine when I allow my spirit...

To lead with my heart guide, my gutsiness to stand up to the challenges, keeping my mind focused and from over-thinking; the mind's eye laser focused on my opulent utopian upshots...

As I now understand I encompass the doubtless clout to experience life my way in a baby bold way, to see what I am willing to sit through to get to the comfort zone...

Of my wealth and success because I now realize my subconscious imprint paychecks were to realize paychecks take a lot of heart and humility to obtain because of all the humanness...

That is occurred to ensure the paycheck; I opened my eyes to get paid a 40=hour paycheck while putting in about 55-60 hours per week through commutes – get up, get ready, be there before start time...

Entertains my thoughts; people in power forget people have lives and a job is a way to pay bills and keep life moving this country; life has moved away from family into being paycheck puppets putting...

More effort into their jobs and the way they make money than they way they treat family; as I realize this it me sets me free: How is the reader of this book as they open their prime time admission? I have submitted...

To being a paycheck puppet without realizing it...Geez...Please, I authorize me to be FREE to realize any word spoken about work is a waste pasting me on the wall and stalling all my dreams...

All this dissing of my dreams ends now because a paycheck is the payer's comfort zone; the payee is endeared to the payer, sending the payee into wondering what is going to happen...

This day and time I am unwinding my wisdom innovation to live MY WAY; I understand there will be challenges and chaos for me to emboss and toss out of my life right after...

I obtain my wisdom, valor and visionary vitality to invoke revolutionary reality; to relish residing

inside my lavish luxury because I now grasp
lavish luxury...

I do what I desire, embellishing a sassy smile on
face to unlace my place on the world stage of
success – now and forever – in a robust right
way; in a luminary loving way; in a bold,
blessed way; under grace in a proud, loud,
perfect way; and, in soulful Divine order NOW!

I Am a Troublemaker for God Sakes

I am a troublemaker for God Sakes; as I opened
my eyes to grasp my Founding Fathers were
called troublemakers by the King of England for
God Sakes, I instantly kicked the fake and
bake...

Out the door; now I take my troublemaker fame
to heart, fanning autonomous majestic
emancipation across this nation;
sensationalizing I am a frontrunner facilitator of
my wily will...

To expand the world by mirroring my Founding
Father's foresight; because I am a sovereign
campaigner for God Sakes, I unbridle my rabble
rousing go-getter...

To dart daring, audacious resolve – tantalizing
intra-ballsy to slam dunk the punks of poverty –
to boldly show me I am free to mirror my
Founding Fathers' stroll to open a new world...

I embellish and relish today because I am a
mischief-maker in my herd; I unsheathe my
sword of sapience to cut through hysteria,
mundane malaria, engaging my raging
sagaciousness...

To romp across the Universe with stubbornness;
I unmask my intrepid explorer because I
encompass the guts to reveal my stouthearted
soul mirroring...

Of what my Founding Fathers were willing to
do; I release my classy savvy, unfurling
stainless lithe, enflaming my willpower to
shower the earth's ethers with emblazoned
audacity...

As I am open to do, I unleash whirlwinds of
wild 'how do you do woo' that emboldens my
wisdom, omnipotent omnificence to undo the
sheep pooh of 'what am to do in this era?'...

Smearing fear of, 'oh, what is the economy
going to do?' These questions stop here because
I now unleash my – I am troublemaker for God
Sakes – visionary with vibrant innovative
freedoms...

Unlatching my panache to unhook the duping of
me, a world of quackery that UN-teaches culture
and preaches of society's insanity – I got you by
gaucheness – as I was told...

To fit in with paradox thinking outside of the
box; it is a crock of crap – strapping my
subliminal mind to this ridiculous rhetoric – that
is now sleeping in oblivion; so now I
unscramble my new rambling resolve...

To cognize that I am a troublemaker; I exited
thinking outside the box crock to sashay in a
sphere of sunlit wit...

I have been and always will be called a
troublemaker because I choose to stand up for
my internal integrity; I find the layoff list first
because I choose to stand for something
rather...

Than slither, dither and wither, to stay
someplace as I lack the courage to stand for
convictions; instead, I introduced me to my
mischief-maker magician...

I watch my ringleader's zealous energy flow
into my rivers of resolve, reveres my effrontery
stouthearted luminary visionary, expanding...

People's will to see their own entrepreneurial
talents, quaking paltry ways folks see the world
spiraling into fear because they see their way of
life diminishing in quick way...

So, as I stroll through life in free troublemaker
spirit, opening people's hearts and eyes to see
their innovative ingenuity, dissing their fears
like a pair of old shoes – I allow people to stroll
through life...

In a free troublemaker spirit I see my
provocative prowess and I open my warrior eyes
to my intra-rising enterpriser to see that the

world is asking for my individual residual resolve...

To solve the world challenges because the way peoples' lives have hit a wall, stalling because people want to change but fear the exploration of expanding through life...

As I untaught myself the pain of change in order to step in the batter box of understanding, expanding is grand, generating robust awesomeness and naturalizing the discerning yearning...

To expand my life; this invigorates my stalwart stand to understand that my wisdom spins the world on its axis of awesomeness, as I see my inner spree and celebrate my daily escapades...

Celebration un-buzzes, it unhooks me from being snookered into society's silliness because I have opened my heart and eyes to my firebrand purity; I let go of societal security and expanded out of fitting in...

Expanded into my heart hierophant's foresight, energizing my firefighter feistiness to understand that to expand out of something, I must muster the monster might to tell the inner fright...

To take long hike on very short plank...because I am a troublemaker for God Sakes; I innately

blow the whistle on society's fouls of frivolous,
ominous, usury lechery as I whistle...

My tune of whimsical, harmonious, intuitive,
savvy, thaumaturgic, luminosity electrifying my
Wi-Fi giant to be defiantly different, to engage
mediocrity of the social system-ocrisy...

I must 'fit in to win' is a fascist fallacy raising
hell with my hallowed energy loving life, so
now I unleash my, I am a troublemaker for God
Sakes, on fascist fallacies; I untangle...

My Founding Fathers wrangle to ride the
tornado of incorruptible listening, to hear the
people asking for the unmasking of their intra-
seer in order to walk their paths of prosperity...

Brazenly, this beams my wise, audacious,
laudable, kevalin wisdom from within my skin;
I am the unraveling rebel uncluttering people's
karmic clutter...

Because I am my intra-troublemaker for God
Sakes; un-puttering my karmic pollution to
expand the world, I choose to quake my inner
quackery with my firebrand of rhymes to
telecast...

I encompass the sand to stand in the fires of
hell, tumultuously unwinding my divine diviner
to shine from within – to win my game of
emancipation from my puttering clutter is now
in the gutter...

As I am THEE Troublemaker for God Sakes; to ride my tides of prosperity by gliding in my seventh heaven shows me that I am the Divine connoisseur of self-assured astuteness...

Because the troublemaker I enjoyed for God Sakes was my internal revolutionary boldness to free my eternal soul – to send out unconditional love...

To expand people's innovative intuition by utilizing my Founding Father's Farsightedness through my own emotional intra-prizing essence...

This shows my effervescent, electric sagacity to live and reside in my lavish luxury...in a bold new way; in an unselfish, loving way; in a Divine blessed way; under grace in a picture perfect way, and in Divine order, NOW!

Robert A. Wilson

I hope you enjoyed, *I Approve of Me Sets Me Free*. I am Robert Wilson; NLP Practitioner, Hypnotherapist, Past Regression Specialist, Reiki Master, Radio Show Host, Parts Integration and Time Line Coach.

Cowboy Wisdom Radio is on Tuesday and Thursday at 8PM Eastern/5PM Pacific and has reached out to listeners.

www.blogtalkradio.com/cwbywsdm

Cowboy Wisdom Visionary Vitality opens your enterprising listening to unmask your entrepreneurial wise, and unleash your canonized abilities so you see **all** the opulent opportunities to experience your copious outcomes with galvanizing gusto from now to eternity.

Cowboy Wisdom Visionary Vitality shows people how to expand through life with a forward-looking attitude, unleashing people-winning witem by showcasing wisdom, innovation, talent, and energizing mammoth money. It allows people to let go of being attached to money; instead, it teaches people to trust their abilities in order to energize their lavish, never-ending, cascading cash flow from all sources in the universe, in a bold bright way and in Divine order NOW!

Robert A. Wilson

www.cowboy-wisdom.com

rob@cowboy-wisdom.com

cwbywsdm@gmail.com

A SPECIAL THANK YOU TO YOU!

On behalf of everyone at Freedom Of Speech Publishing, thank you for choosing I Approve of Me... Sets me Free for your reading enjoyment.

As an added bonus and special thank you, for purchasing I Approve of Me... Sets me Free, you can enjoy discounts and special promotions on other Freedom of Speech Publishing products. Visit www.freedomeofspeech.com/vip to learn more.

We are committed to providing you with the highest level of customer satisfaction possible. If for any reason you have questions or comments, we are delighted to hear from you. Email us at cs@freedomofspeechpublishing.com or visit our website at: http://freedomofspeechpublishing.com/contact-us-2/.

If you enjoyed I Approve of Me... Sets me Free, visit www.freedomofspeechpublishing.com for a list of similar books or upcoming books.

Again, thank you for your patronage. We look forward to providing you more entertainment in the future.

I Approve of Me... Sets me Free
By Robert A. Wilson

For more books like this one, visit Robert A. Wilson's website at:

http://cowboy-wisdom.com/

2012 copyright by Freedom of Speech Publishing, Inc.

Printed in the United States of America
The publisher offers discounts on this book when ordered in bulk quantities. For more information, contact Sales Department, Phone 815-290-9605, Email:
sales@FreedomOfSpeechPublishing.com

Freedom of Speech Publishing, Leawood KS, 66224
www.FreedomOfSpeechPublishing.com
ISBN: 1938634098
ISBN-13: 978-1-938634-09-3